D1558073

Italia! oh Italia! Thou who hast The fatal gift of beauty...

Lord Byron

Translated from the French by Louise Rogers Lalaurie
Copyediting: Lisa Barnett
Graphic design: Alessandra Scarpa
Art direction: Alain Bouldouyre
Color separation: Compo Juliot

Facing page, clockwise from top:
Essential travel kit:
travel-size Windsor & Newton
  watercolor box
lifeline!
protection against the Evil Eye
cool Italian shades
for energy
indelible ink drawing-pen
hot lipstick
accent to be perfected in situ!

Italian chic

Watercolors by FLORINE ASCH

My Italian Sketchbook

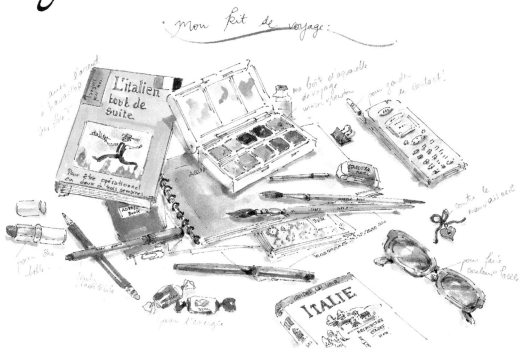

Foreword by DOMINIQUE FERNANDEZ
Notes on the Grand Tour by OLIVIER MESLAY

Flammarion

For Rose

I am grateful to my friends Véronique Prat and Patrick Perrin who, over dinner in 1998, first suggested the idea for a Grand Tour of Italy, following in the footsteps of the eighteenth-century artists who traveled throughout the peninsula, bringing back writings, paintings, and drawings.

For the following two years I explored Italy, watercolor box and sketchbook in hand, with no particular itinerary in mind, stopping whenever I felt inclined to sketch a charming "piazzeta", a splendid Venetian interior, a Tuscan landscape, the unintentionally humorous juxtapositions of a row of shops.

I took along writings on Italy by some of my favorite authors, noting their words in my sketchbooks when they seemed appropriate to the scene depicted, or simply when I was moved by the beauty of the text...

This book contains just some of the hundreds of watercolors from my two-years journey...

Florine

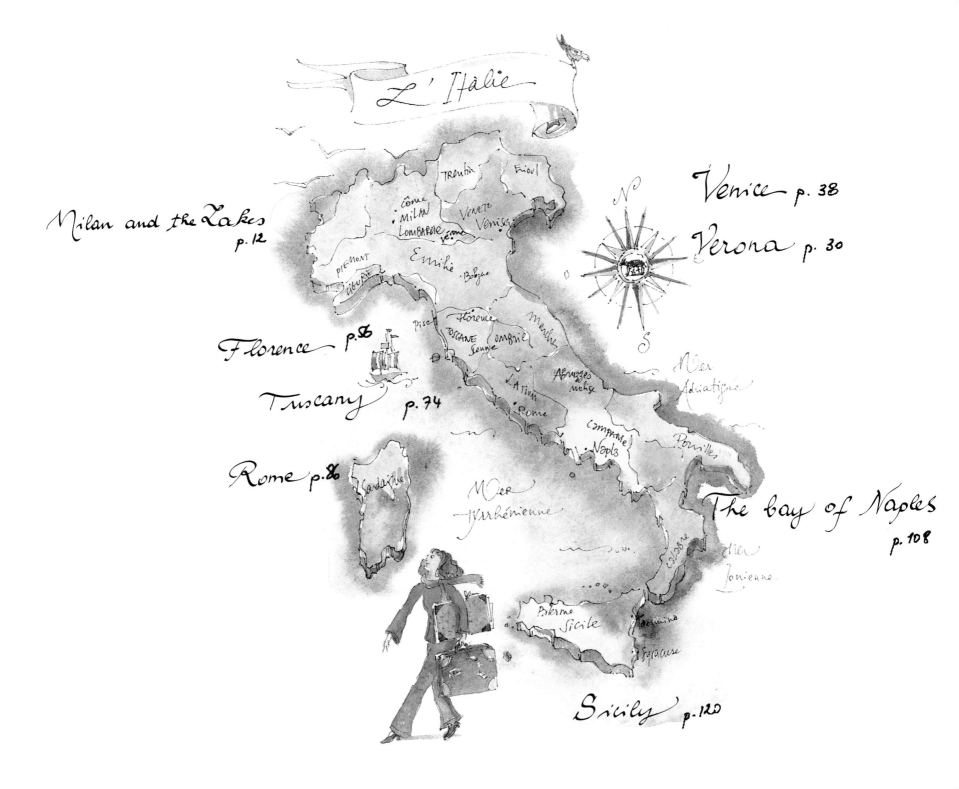

L'Italie

Trentin

Frioul

Côme

MILAN

Venise

LOMBARDIE

Vénétie

Vérone

PIÉMONT

Émilie

Bologne

LIGURIE

Pise

Florence

Marche

TOSCANE

Gênes

OMBRIE

Abruzzes Molise

LATIUM

Rome

Campanie

Naples

Pouilles

Sardaigne

Mer Tyrrhénienne

Mer Adriatique

Calabre

Mer Ionienne

Palerme

Sicile

Taormina

Syracuse

Florine's Grand Tour

by DOMINIQUE FERNANDEZ

A Grand Tour, in the year 2000? In the age of the jumbo jet, when travelers can hop straight from their home cities to Venice, Rome, Naples, or Sicily? We remember the Grand Tour of old with nostalgia, perhaps, but it is very definitely dead, and dead twice over.

It is dead because too few modern travelers trouble to journey from north to south, lingering en route through the changing regions of the Italian peninsula. Today's mass tourists—hurrying against the clock (or the wristwatch) to do as much as possible with their limited time and budgets—are the antithesis of the Grand Tourists of the past, whose travels lasted several months, and sometimes even years. Rather than "do" Venice or Rome on a whistle-stop, one-stop vacation, they would "tour" from one destination to the next, unhurried, unworried, disdaining schedules and timetables, free to go where they pleased, trusting to chance, making the most of the incomparable richness and variety of a country such as Italy. The term "tourist," first coined by the nineteenth-century French writer Stendhal to mean one who travels not to arrive, but aimlessly as the servant of beauty, has become sadly debased.

Rumors of the death of the Grand Tour are not, then, exaggerated. And that death seems somehow much more final—beyond all hope of resurrection—when we remember those twin essentials without which the provisions of any Grand Tourist were hopelessly incomplete: the notebook, of course, but also the sketchbook—indispensable items enabling the traveler to record in words and images the landscapes, cities, and monuments that he (or she) had traversed, visited, and admired. Not all travelers were

accomplished draughtsmen, however. Sir William Hamilton, the English diplomat and connoisseur appointed plenipotentiary to Naples in 1764, was accompanied on his expeditions to Vesuvius by the painter Pietro Fabris, whose gouaches provide us with delightful views of Naples and the surrounding countryside. The Marquis de Sade's artistic adviser in Rome and Naples was the painter Jean-Baptiste Tierce, whose sketchbook is the essential companion to Sade's *Voyage d'Italie*. The first traveler of importance to illustrate his own writings was none other than Goethe, whose two-year tour (1786–1788) took him from Venice to Sicily by way of Rome and Naples, then home via Florence and Milan. The great writer produced a multitude of drawings, watercolors, and sketches in wash and sepia, with a particular fondness for the monuments of antiquity and for bucolic landscapes evocative of Virgil. Karl Friedrich Schinkel, the great nineteenth-century German architect, undertook two Italian Grand Tours—first in 1803, to Venice and Sicily via Bologna, Florence, Rome, and Naples, and again in 1824, from Milan to Assisi via Genoa, Pisa, Florence, and Perugia, complementing his travel journal with a wealth of drawings and watercolors. But it is in the travel sketches of Eugène Viollet-le-Duc that Florine Asch's work finds its most direct forerunner. The future champion of French Romantic architecture traveled to Italy as a young man, from 1836 to 1837, taking in Genoa and Sicily on the journey out, and returning via Rome and Venice. We have no grandiloquent travelogue, but simply his letters home, expressing his personal "traveler's creed": "When you live, as I have done

Coupe XVᵉ siècle ornée de pierreries.
Collection de Laurent Le Magnifique

Fifteenth-century goblet, set with gemstones
Laurent the Magnificent collection

pierres précieuses

cristal de Roche

émail

argent

for the past eighteen months, surrounded by nothing but works of art, all these monuments, these sculptures, these columns speak to you in a language of their own; they are more than friends, they are lovers; and I love to see them, to study them, to know their intimate charms and details, to feel their closeness. In their presence, one can forget about life…", but not the duty to sketch them for the record. With quill pen and Indian ink, in wash, gouache, and watercolor, the twenty-two-year-old novice harvested a wealth of images. Drawing, he noted (and I feel sure that Florine Asch would agree) could be more than a "leisurely diversion." It was rather an effort of the intellect, an attempt to represent "thought incarnate." Eschewing what he called "easy, picturesque" views of the familiar architectural ensembles, the young architect focused instead on details. Only here, he felt, could one find "the dominant effect, the main impression that fixes itself indelibly upon the spirit". The lines might have been written with our own young traveler in mind; yet today, Viollet-le-Duc's advice seems to have been taken up most assiduously by practitioners of photography, the quick-fire art that has (largely) supplanted drawing for the modern traveler. All too often, today's tourist has no time to sit at the base of a column, sketchbook on knees. He simply trains his lens on landscapes and monuments, takes (or plunders) a multitude of pictures, and returns home with a superficial hoard of "instant snapshots." We may know how to take a picture, but that does not make us masters of the art of photography. We peer through the viewfinder rather than experience reality at first hand; we avoid looking in depth at what we see around us and are content simply to record, reproduce, and hoard it by mechanical means. We have

precious stones
rock crystal
enamel
silver

lost "the means to record our observations in the true lan-guage of the soul". The Grand Tour provided an unparal-leled opportunity to experience "the intellectual dialog between the model and the hand". Drawing unites the hand and the intel-lect in a challenging but spiritually rewarding endeavor—a truly outmoded notion in our era of instant gratification. Without time, there can be no drawing; in the absence of both, the death of the Grand Tour was inevitable.

In this context, Florine Asch's work is little short of miraculous. After specializing in decorative art—producing illustrations and drawings for books, greetings cards, lampshades, menus, and tableware (developing a confident, spontaneous style with great economy of line and a lively use of color)—this talented thirty-year-old French artist has chosen to follow in the footsteps of some of her most illustrious forebears, traveling like Viollet-le-Duc and Goethe from Milan to Sicily via Venice, Florence, Rome, and Naples. The most challenging task was to salvage some shred of the former beauty of that most industrialized, overdeveloped, and disfigured of Italian cities, Milan—so beloved of Stendhal that he declared himself to be *Milanese*, but with seemingly little to detain the latter-day tourist. In the galleries of Classical Greek casts in the city's plasterworks, in the Baroque chapels of the Duomo and the Church of Sant' Ambrogio, or in a corner of the iron-and-glass Galleria—every bit as symbolic of its time as the emphat-ic, triumphal operas of Verdi—Florine Asch finds an elegant solution. Milan deserves to be included, and not simply out of deference to its past or pity for its present predicament. In Venice, the problem was turned on its

head: how does one express something fresh and new amid so much familiar (even potentially tiresome) beauty? Asch's approach is simple and straightforward. Her watercolors of the Café Florian, haunted by the shades of Casanova and Proust, or a carriage of the Orient Express rich with marquetry and nostalgia (for fans of Paul Morand and Agatha Christie), recall her work for the luxury hotels, restaurants, and shops of Paris. Nor has she neglected the Grand Canal, the Dogana di Mare, the island of San Giorgio, or even the Doge's Palace, rendering the famous settings with poetic economy and the lightest of touches. One sketch features deferential borrowings from the works of the Venetian master Carpaccio: a gondolier's back (as in the cycle painted for the Scuola di S. Orsola) and a little dog (from the cycle for the Scuola San Giorgio degli Schiavoni).

Tuscany was, it seems, a source of particular inspiration for Florine—the sketches perfectly capture the limpid skies, the delicate silhouettes of *campanile* outlined against the horizon, and the dry, airy grace of the countryside, punctuated with cypress trees and dotted with pink villas. In the antique shops and couture boutiques of Florence—Gucci, Versace, Valentino—Asch is on familiar territory, rediscovering the urban sophistication and polish of her earlier work for the likes of Hermès and Cartier in Paris. Asch's work is suffused with the warm, open-hearted appetite for life that is essential if the Grand Tour is not to become a dreary litany of visits to museums and cemeteries (as was the case, on occasion, with such ponderous predecessors as Goethe, Chateaubriand, and Henry James). Capturing the profusion of venison sausages, wild boar hams, Chianti flasks, and cheese mountains in the *Bazar dei Sapor*—a gastronomic Ali Baba's cave in San Gimignano—or the bustling life and color in a Sienese market, Asch delights in the Italian people themselves: as lively, engaging, and full of fun as the sketches in this book.

On to Rome, and the solemn burden of history. Or rather, the tiny houses clustering around Campo dei Fiori, a mule waiting for tourists in front of the Trevi Fountain, the broken remains of a few antique columns—all are captured by the same deft brush that renders a dog, a cat, modern Romans out for a bracing stroll, a line of washing, a griffon standing guard over the city's domes, and sea gods blowing vigorously into conch shells beside the flower stalls of the Piazza Navone. Asch's street scenes plunge the viewer into the daily lives of the Roman *popolino*, the "little people" whose humor and liveliness are the perfect complement to her privileged glimpses of the city's grand aristocratic salons. Like Stendhal before her, Asch knows the true secret of the Grand Tour: to be equally at home in a formal palace interior and a bustling Roman street, to admire what is beautiful without losing the zest for everyday life, to depict the lyrical and the mischievous with the same natural touch.

Last, but not least, to the south. It is more ragamuffin than haute couture—its economy lagging behind the prosperous north—but rich in poetic beauty. The raw brilliance of Naples is a far cry from the elegance of Florence or Rome; yet, transformed by Asch's graceful, confident drawing and smart, bright colors, the narrow streets barred with lines of dancing laundry look for all the

world like a shop window on the rue du Faubourg Saint-Honoré. Here, too, is Florine's marvelous view of the little port of Mergellina, the Riviera di Chiaia (the seafront promenade that is also Naples's public park), and the Castell dell'Ovo, which is not stifled by the noisy bustle of an over-populated metropolis, but as if freshly risen from the sea, framed by a clump of palm trees and the double cone of Vesuvius.

And so to Sicily, where in addition to the expected and skillfully executed homages to the antique theatre at Taormina and the San Domenico Palace Hotel (the "Mediterranean Ritz"), Asch has succeeded in capturing other less familiar aspects of the island's life and charm: the Baroque splendor of the church of San Giorgio di Ragusa; the facades of Noto or a balcony in Palermo; picturesque markets; and families thrilling to the adventures of the comical *pupi*, strutting the stages of their tiny puppet theatres to reenact scenes of love and war from the great Italian epic romances—Ariosto's *Orlando Furioso* or Tasso's *Gerusalemme Liberata* (*Jerusalem Delivered*).

Florine's journey is a scrupulous reenactment of the old Grand Tour, an exemplary exploration of Italy's treasures, undertaken with little more than a box of Windsor & Newton watercolors, an indelible ink drawing-pen, brushes, pencil, rubber, an amulet to ward off the Evil Eye, an open heart, and—most important of all—a quick eye and confident hand with which to record her impressions, observations, and adventures.

"These Leicas, these Zeiss; do people no longer have eyes?"

Paul Morand, *Venices*

The Grand Tour, an historical note ...

by OLIVIER MESLAY

In the early seventeenth century Anthony Ashley Cooper, third earl of Shaftesbury, defined the essential attainments of an educated and enlightened gentleman. These included an informed, unerring artistic taste, which, being acquired rather than innate, needed to be forged and cultivated. Italy was the country for the job, hence the fashion among the English gentry for sending their offspring on long tours of the Italian peninsula, initially to Florence and Rome, then increasingly to Venice and Naples. To the English aristocracy, Italian travel became an art and their journeys, the stuff of legend. The term "Grand Tour" was quickly coined from the French. Today's humble "tourist" owes his title to the Grand Tourists of old. Yet these English travelers were anything but humble. Some, like Lord Burlington, traveled with a sizeable retinue; others, more simply, but still in considerable style. French aristocrats followed suit, including the future Marquis de Marigny (brother of Madame de Pompadour), architect Germain Soufflot, and painter Charles Nicolas Cochin.

The eighteenth century was, then, mesmerized by Italy and Italian antiquities. Italy was seen as the fountainhead of culture and civilization, from the great classics of Latin literature to Dante and Boccacio, along with the masterpieces of Roman statuary, widely held to be the embodiment of beauty and the source of the aesthetic canon. Travelers flocked to the Italian cities, drawn by the works of the great Renaissance and Bolognese masters. English monarch George III, unfit to make the journey, commissioned artist Johann Zoffany to paint a single work containing the essential highlights of the trip. The result was the extraordinary *Tribuna of the Uffizi*, which included not only the main masterpieces from Florence's Uffizi museum, but also a selection of works from elsewhere and, of course, large numbers of English tourists admiring them. Despite Zoffany's best efforts, such a work could never truly convey the scenes that continue to enchant travelers to Italy today: landscapes bathed in the peninsula's unique light or a monument struck by a shaft of sunshine. Hence the great popularity among travelers of views of Venice by Canaletto (whose chief patron was Joseph Smith, appointed English consul in Venice in 1744), Vanvitelli's views of Rome, and Neapolitan scenes by the painter Lusieri. Travelers to Rome immortalized their visit with a portrait by the society artist Pompeo Batoni, who invariably pictured his subjects against a background of Roman monuments or with some antique treasure from the papal collections.

The Grand Tour and all things Italian became so fashionable, so utterly *de rigeur*, that one of London's most select clubs, the so-called *Dilettanti*, recruited members exclusively from the ranks of those who had not only made the journey, but returned suitably enlightened, and were prepared to devote themselves to promoting the music, painting, and culture of their adoptive "second home." The club provided travel grants for artists. From the mid-eighteenth century, a number of notable English sculptors and painters made the Grand Tour, including Reynolds, Flaxman, and Wright of Derby, to name but a few.

The passage of time did nothing to diminish this influx of English travelers, but it did alter its course. Eighteenth-century artists were drawn to the brilliant light of the south, but Turner, in the nineteenth century, never revisited Rome once he had fallen under the spell of Venice. Times changed, and with them, the tastes of the patrons whose travels resulted in the fine collections of Italian art still to be admired in so many English country houses. The grand compositions of Guide and the Carracci brothers fell from favor, and the gold backgrounds and painted saints of another, perhaps less enlightened, age took their place. From the end of the nineteenth century, even contemporary artists eschewed modernity in favor of the Pre-Raphaelite.

The Grand Tour goes on, and artists continue to absorb and be dazzled by the spectacle of Italy. Florine Asch follows in the footsteps of many other youthful painters seeking to capture its special beauty. Like Italy itself, her pictures are suffused with an irresistible, infectious *joie de vivre*. And like so many other Grand Tour artists, watercolor is her medium of choice. No other medium is better suited to capture the traveler's fleeting impressions, but speed of execution demands absolute accuracy. A watercolor either succeeds on the spot, or is thrown away. That is its greatest value, as proved by the deceptive ease, faultless execution, and enormous charm of the paintings in this book.

Gallery of views of Ancient Rome. Pannini. XVIII th century

Dear Florine,

Milan has gone mad. For three days each year, the city explodes with joy in celebration of the Feast of St. Ambrose, and his protection of the Lombard capital. Around the basilica containing the saint's remains there is a market setting up, with rare books, old prints, incense and lucky charms, pastries and doughnuts, jewelry, hot chestnuts, balloons . . .

The crowds are already thronging onto Piazza Sant'Ambrogio. Just once a year, Milan looks like the casbah at Djema el Fnaa! I adore this period in Advent, with its strange alliance of Christian culture and ancient pagan rites.

When you come next week we'll take tea together at Ambroeus on the corso Matteotti, just off the via Montenapoleone. You'll love their irresistible old-fashioned Italian pastries. At this time of year, you can already buy the fabulous stuffed *panettone* for Christmas.

In the plush hush of the smartest Milanese homes, the staff uniforms are still bedecked with starched lace, and children grow up swathed in cashmere and flannel under the indulgent, if sometimes rather intrusive, gaze of their grandmothers. The mothers, for their part, devote themselves to their careers or their little dogs (with peculiar passion, in the latter case). Most Milanese dogs have extraordinarily aristocratic pedigrees, and are treated accordingly.

We shall go window shopping along via Montenapoleone. You will notice the often disaffected, dissatisfied look of ladies in splendid boutiques sporting patent crocodile handbags. Then I shall take you to the Papiniano market in Sant'Agostino, the quarter around the church of Sant'Ambrogio. You find the most delicious regional Italian produce here: fragrant Sicilian lemons, capers from Lipari, extra-virgin olive oil from Tuscany, Neapolitan mozzarella, and lentils from Ventotene. Such a mixture of smells and tastes!

In Milan, fewer and fewer people are Milanese "born and bred"; but everyone—Neapolitans,

December 7th, 1999

Florentines, Romans, Bolognese, Venetians—
conforms to the one essential criterion for
acceptance: productivity. True, Italy is more often
drawn to the labors of Venus than of Hercules, but
Milan is the exception. The Milanese extremely
driven, often working fourteen or fifteen hours a
day. Working for two years with Franco Maria Ricci
in the majestic publishing house on via
Monteccuocoli has been a truly joyous experience
for me. I am so pleased to be able to take you around
this extraordinary, baroque place during your visit to
Milan. It is the artistic memory of Italy.

   One day, in his office, a distinguished French
visitor asked me, "Are you in Italy for your work?"
No, *monsieur*. I am in Italy for love.

To our loves and our laughter, dear Florine!
See you soon in Milan.

Estelle Arielle Bouchet

Galleria Victor Emmanuel
154 ft (47 meters) high

Maurizio's dressing room

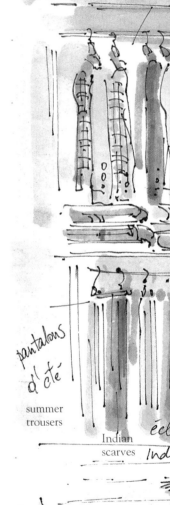

Andrea Pfister

Te va a pennello!

satin

feathers

perles
Brodées

embroidered with pearls

pantalons d'été

summer
trousers

Indian
scarves

Ferragamo

perles

swan's down

Salvatore
Ferragamo

14

de Maurizio

r jackets

vestes du soir

dinner
jackets

Che gusti vuoi? : stracciatella
pistacchio
nocciola

malaga
limone
fragola
cioccolata
fior di panna ....

The cast workshops

Plasterworks on via Montello

December 4th, 1999

" If the Renaissance placed Man at the center of the universe,
the Baroque put statuary at the center of art.
In squares and fountains, in gardens, on rooftops, in churches
and palaces, marble, bronze, stone and giltwood reach out,
spiraling and soaring, between earth and sky, in
billowing clouds of drapery and incense..."
    J.N Schifano, "Désirs d'Italie".

    The Duomo. Milan

Buste
marbre

papc en
Bois
XVIIe n.

Sarcophage
Egyptien

table
drapé en
Bois trompe l'œil!

Milan. the office of the
publisher Franco Maria Ricci

Bellagio

The Hotel Villa d'Este on Lake Como

Lake Como

Verona

Palazzo Maffei

Verona

Juliet: How camest thou hither, tell me,
      and wherefore?
   The orchard walls are high and hard to climb;
   And the place death, considering who thou art,
   If any of my kinsmen find thee here.

Romeo: With love's light wings did I o'erperch
   these walls;
   For stony limits cannot hold love out,
   And what love can do, that dares love attempt.
   Therefore thy kinsmen are no stop to me ...

        Shakespeare. Romeo and Juliet
        Act II, Scene II

September 29th, 1999

"Sant' Andrea" chez Astrid

"The marketplace, laden with watermelons, lemons, limes and tomatoes.... The houses, colored with frescoes by Paolo Albasini, have the most romantic features: Soaring watchtowers, ornamental sculpture, robust pillars. Columns with intricate capitals are the finishing touch, making the square a marvelous subject for watercolorists and decorators."

T. Gauthier

Legendary headgear. Borsalino, Piazza delle Erbe

"Now and again would appear a handsomer building that happened to be there like a surprise in a box one has just opened, a little ivory temple with its Corinthian columns and an allegorical statue on its pediment, somewhat out of place among the ordinary surroundings in the midst of which, for all that we tried to make space for it, the peristyle with which the canal had provided it retained the look of a landing-stage for market gardeners ..."

Marcel Proust. "A la recherche du Temps Perdu". La fugitive

November 6th, 1999

Venice

View of the Salute

Basilica di San Marco

"When the first motorboat speeds
past, the reflections of mooring
posts look like crooked,
Solomonic columns."

Paul Morand, "Venices"

November 7th, 1999

"La stagion del Carnevale
tutto el mondo fa cambiar.
Chi sta bene e chi sta male
Carnaval fa rallegrar.

Chi ha denari se li spende;
chi non ne ha, ne vuol trovar;
e s'impegna, e poi si vende,
per andarsi a sollazzar.

Qua la moglie e là il marito,
ognun va dove gli par;
ognun corre a qualque invito,
chi a giocare e chi a ballar"

c. Goldoni, la mascherata

Le maschere della commedia dell'arte ...

Capitan Spezzaferro   La Cantatrice   Fritellino   Leandro   Meo Patacca

Waders borrowed
from the Gritti

Bottes voulants
prêtés par
le gritti

Patrick place St. Marc
Aquà Altà + pluie + neige

Patrick, St Mark's Square
Aquà Altà + rain + snow

" The houses of Venice are buildings that have nostalgic
longing to be boats. That is why their ground floors are
often flooded. They are satisfying their fondness for a
permanent home as well as their nomadic instincts
    Paul Morand "Venice"

November 22ᵈ, 1999

"l'aqua Alta"
Aquà Altà

the house
specialty:
coffee,
chocolate,
cream…

Petit Déjeuner au Florian

Breakfast at Café Florian

47

Antique shop, Piazza San Toma, Venice

Venice. Ca' Brazadin The cats keep me company

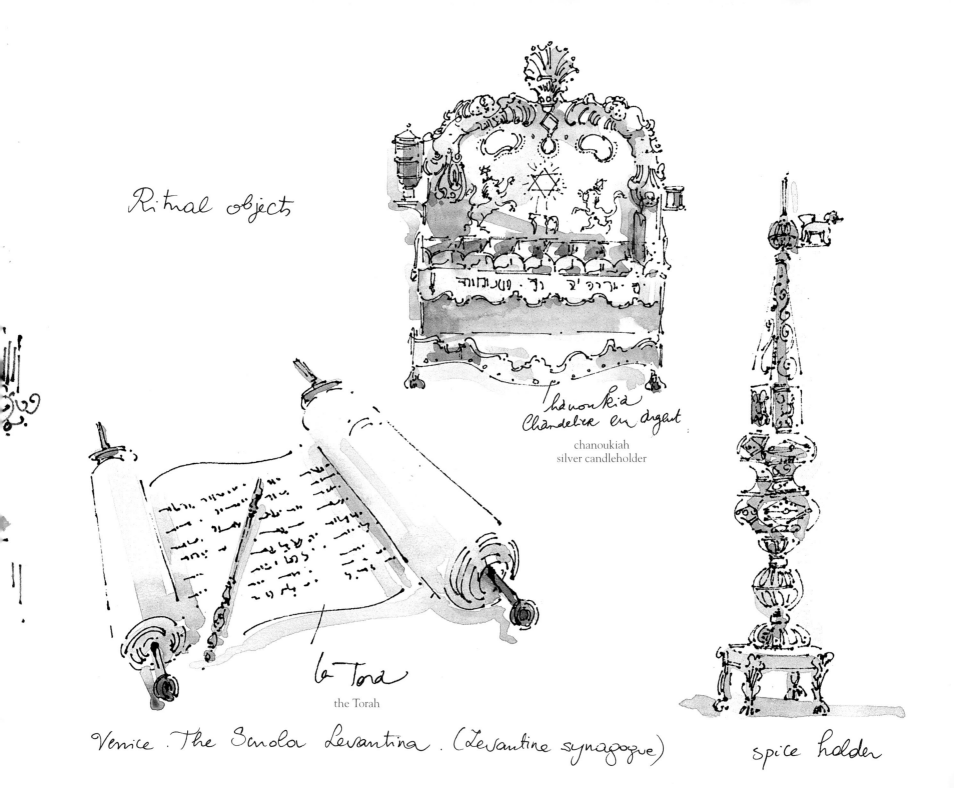

Ritual objects

chanoukia
Chandelier en argent

chanoukiah
silver candleholder

la Tora

the Torah

Venice. The Scuola Levantina. (Levantine synagogue)

spice holder

"A moment later, a door in the corner of the room opened to admit a beautiful woman, her face covered by a velvet mask, irregular rather than oval in shape, known in Venice as a "Moretta". The appearance of this mask surprised and enchanted the assembled company, for it was indeed impossible to imagine a more fascinating object, as much for the beauty of its form, as for the elegance of its setting."

Giacomo Casanova. "The story of my life"

November 23rd, 1999

November 24th, 1999
Back from Venice aboard
the Orient Express . . .
the dining car
marquetry, tropical
hardwoods

"Lend me your deafening racket, your smooth-running speed,
Your nocturnal snaking through Europe and its lights,
O luxury sleeper! And the agonizing music
That plays out along your corridors of gilded hide
While behind the lacquered doors, the bright, brass-heavy latches
The millionaires are sleeping soundly."
        Valery Larbaud. Ode

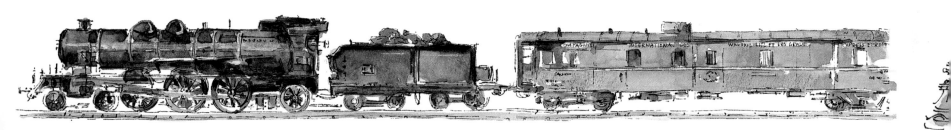

on 99
2 de Venise
ient Express...
u Salle à manger
etrie de
precieux.

marqueterie de Bois

marquetry

acajou

mahogany

the Swiss Alps

velours vert

green velvet

vaisselle
& verre
grand
pour
orient Ex

Orient Express tableware and
specially engraved glasses

Florence

Florence   An Italian colleague, Piazza dello Signoria

Florence. Le marché
Market, Florence

Florence Borgo San Jacopo

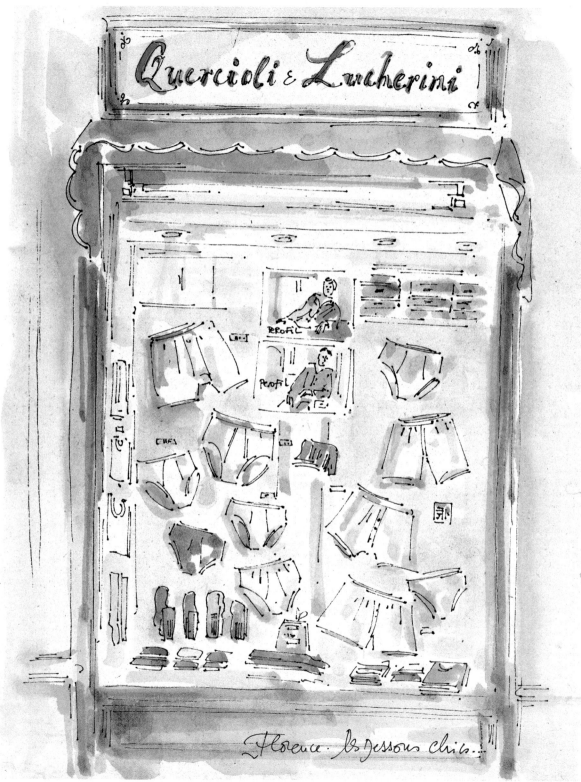

Florentine chic. His . . .

BIANCHERIA *Henrietta* REGGISENO

16

. . . and hers.

candy jars

July 31st, 1998

L'officina profumo farmaceutica di Santa Maria Novella is one of the oldest pharmacies in the world. The decor is sumptuous; frescoes and old-fashioned shop-fittings and instruments.

enteries Florentines.

Florentine home accessories

Gucci, Prada...

Vuitton etc.

Luxury goods on the ponte Vecchio

Tenue de pluie. Florence

Florence in the rain

The cast collection and antiques at G. Turchi, via Maggio

allegoria
de la scultura

La justi
XVII

San
giovanni
Alabastro
17e.

candelabro
Sicilia
XVIIIe s.

gesso per una fontana
1920

Argent
1887

Les œufs de

Easter

April 22nd, 2000

marocchino:
a macchiato sprinkled
with cocoa powder

Florence 11 a.m.
Coffee break

Coffee may be ordered:
ristretto : "short", strong and black
lungo : "longer", diluted (black)
doppio : a "double", (black)
con panna: with whipped cream
Caffé macchiato : espresso with a (very) little milk
latte macchiato : a ristretto poured over hot milk (in a glass)

Pasta fresca
Ravioli Canuti

OLIO di OLIVA
Extra Vergine

Chianti
Classico

made in Italy

Mon ancêtre peinte à Florence par Gomek XIXᵉˢ.

My ancestor, painted in Florence by Gomek, XIXth century

The splendid gardens of the Villa Gamberaia in Settignano

chic boutiques in Florence

quelques boutiques chic!.... Firenze

San gimignano

"The rows of trees in the orchards,
the lines of vine-stocks
in the vineyards, perfectly accentuate
the curves, the ridges,

the shifting perspective, the shape
of this sumptuous tapestry,
so that the landscape

resembles a line drawing,
it is engraved rather than painted."

g. Piroué : "J'avais franchi les monts"

August 1st. 1998

my room with a view....

pain toste de Sienne

Toscane
Borgo San Felice
15.04.2000

Tuscany, Borgo San Felice
April 15th, 2000

P. M. A

Roux

Lucca

bazar dei sapori

à San Gimignano

La campagne Toscane The Tuscan countryside

A dream of Siena

The Campo is bathed in morning sunlight. The famous, amphitheater-shaped medieval piazza is not overrun by tourists, yet. A young woman appears at the bottom of the Gothic tower, drawing-pad in hand. She sits at a café terrace, spreading her watercolor box, pencils and brushes over the little table. The artist starts to draw. After a while, she closes her eyes and dreams of the *palio*, Siena's extraordinary sixteenth-century horse-race, when the city's districts (the *contrade*) competed with fevered rivalry. Suddenly, she is startled from her reverie by the deafening sound of hundreds of trumpets. Before her eyes, a colorful crowd invades the piazza. Dozens of men in silk and velvet costumes, some with breastplates, parade across the cobblestones. Each of the ten horses represents one *contrada*. Their riders brandish banners, standards and halberds. A triumphal float bearing the *palio* itself (the banner presented to the winner) brings up the rear. And the mad, violent horse-race begins. Urged on by the clamoring crowds, the mounts and their riders hurtle around the sloping piazza in a whirlwind of color, light, dust, and noise. The first horse home wins, carrying off the *palio*, regardless of how many rivals he has knocked out of the race. The artist opens her eyes. The piazza is deserted. She puts away her watercolors and gets up to leave, when she notices a piece of silk, discarded on the ground: the *palio*. She picks it up, slips it into her pocket and walks away, smiling. The dream has come true.

Roger Auque

paggio maggiore del leocorno

Paggio maggiore dell'aquila

paggio maggiore del drago

Souvenirs
of Siena!

Rome

Piazza del Pantheon.

Dolce vita at the Trevi Fountain

13.02.2000

From the base of the monument to Victor Emmanuel II

View from my room. Campo dei Fiori

Temple of Apollo Sosiano

The "Snow White and the Seven Dwarves" children's hairdressing salon. Via Metastasio. The animal seats are from old fairground rides.

Toys, dolls, boats and balls...

The Palazzo Pallavicini Rospigliosi. Rome. Ancestral portraits.

Chez Michele, Piazza Farnese

A Day in Rome

by Manuel Burrus

Waking up in Rome is never a problem—the scooter-riders see to that! Throw open the shutters: the burning light pierces the eyes, a deafening clamor rises from the street. Not a moment to lose. Down to the street, the great theater of Latin life. Forget the museums, the tourist guides explaining how to do Rome in four days. Take Stendhal's advice and explore at leisure. The Eternal City awaits, with its Antique monuments, its thousand churches, its fifty palaces overflowing with frescoes (apart from one that houses a cinema), its superb villas nestling in the seclusion of their parks, its bridges decorated with statues straddling the lazy waters of the Tiber, its multitude of fountains—from the simple Fontanella di Borghese to the Fontana Trevi, bursting with Baroque triumphalism and *joie de vivre*, Bernini's horses frozen in perpetuity, rearing before the startling beauty of the swooning Anita Ekberg. But Rome is more than this…. It should be visited, *gelato* in hand, in late spring, as the days draw out, when the tables of the cafés and trattorias invade the sidewalks, elbow-to-elbow with antiques from the dealer next door. The light intensifies, reviving the ocher facades newly-washed for the Jubilee. Saint Peter's is a confection of icing-sugar once more; the Farnese Palace no longer that dark, rather terrifying, fortress looming like a giant ocean liner at the end of Campo dei Fiori. Return to the city center in late afternoon, with the crowds of young people thronging the streets around the Spanish Steps. Climb up to Pincio and the Villa Medicis. Rome is spread at your feet. In the foreground, the domes of St Peter's and San Carlo in Corso reach heavenwards as if in prayer. To the left, the Baroque facade of San Ignacio stands proudly, *ad majorem Dei gloriam*. And everywhere, there are terraces overrun with greenery. In the golden light of evening, when— as Dante put it—"the heart softens", let us surrender to the city's unexpected charms, to its elegance at once grand and simple, to priceless jewels lightly worn, and to the intoxicating scent of the mantle of all the ages. Eyes closed, let us taste the sweet, slow poison of the *dolce vita*.

July 2000

Chz La Sforza Cesarini

mon chocolat chaud
délicieux!

RISERVATO

Rome. Le Café Greco

Le Palais Farnèse, La salle des Carrache

Farnese Palace, Carracci room

May 3rd, 2000

"He who does not love the Baroque, cannot love Italy.
Italy, a thousand times transcendent. All is theatre, solemnity, ritual.
Exuberance, turbulence, opulence.
Volutes, arabesques, frienzied spiraling, pathetic puffery.
This is art modeled on grandiloquent excess, in speech and
gesture, in life itself."
                    Georges Mathieu

Piazza Navona

View of St. Peter's

Capella de San Filippo Neri

14.02.2000

The bay of

Naples

The Bay of Naples

Pompeii

Pompeii
La maison du Faune

March 16th, 1999

"Naples is black and bare. Naples, with its din and squalor,
appears barbaric to the traveler who comes down from Rome
although no other city on the peninsula is so subtle, ingenious
or civilized. No other town is so like a capital, especially
if it is compared with Rome. But it has always been
mysteriously swindled of the success that its natives'
talents ought to have won for it. It is a puzzling town,
whose population has the most amazing resources of intelligence
and yet has never found the means of making them bear fruit.

Dominique Fernandez ".The Mother Sea"

Spacca Napoli / Le ghiacchiere

Neapolitan figures. XVIIIth century

Sedi PERRINI

NAPOLI - Palermo (6)

marchand de chaises
dans le vieux Naples

Chair-seller, Old Naples

Capri. A la Faukelina. Le 26 mai 1900

Capri

Amalfi

Le Castello d'Ischia

Sicily

Taormina
Vue sur l'Etna

Taormina
View of Etna

July 6th, 2000

"If a man had but one day to spend in Sicily, and
wanted to know what he should see, I would reply without
hesitation : "Taormina".
This one landscape contains nothing less than all that the
human eye, spirit and imagination finds most seductive in
this world, as if it were put here for that very purpose."

Guy de Maupassant

Taormina. Piazza del Duomo

CORSO
UMBERTO

c'st la fête du Patron de
la ville. Ls Charettes siciliennes
sont de sortis.

Traditional Sicilian carts parade in honor of the local patron saint

The entrance to the San
Domenico Palace Hotel,
Taormina

L'entrée du San Domenico . Taormina

Please make up the room!
In the corridors of the San Domenico

SAN DOMENICO
PALACE HOTEL

PIAZZA SAN DOMENICO, 5 - 98039 TAORMINA (ME) - ITALIA - TEL. +39 0942 23 701
FAX +39 0942 62 55 06 - http://www.thi.it - e-mail: san-domenico@thi.it

View from my room, no. 22
July 3rd, 2000

Vue de ma chambre 3 juillet 2000
n° 212

Syracuse. Ortigia

Chiesa San Giorgio
1738.
Ragusa Ibla

Palermo . City of Contrasts...

Palermo
View of the old port of La Cala
Church of San Domenico

Palerme
Vue des Vieux port La Cala
Chiesa di San Domenico

TEATRINO
PALE

Pupi, célèbres marionnettes qui jouaient des maures.....

exploits de Roland, des croisés et

Pupi. Famous marionettes who reenact
the exploits of Orlando, the Crusaders,
the Moors . . .

Sous le vieux Palerme
Lo Vucceri

Old Palermo, Market

Latte Scremate

Olio di Oliva

£1400

Frutti

Tutti Frutti

Gianni Limonia

133

The "nonna" of Palermo

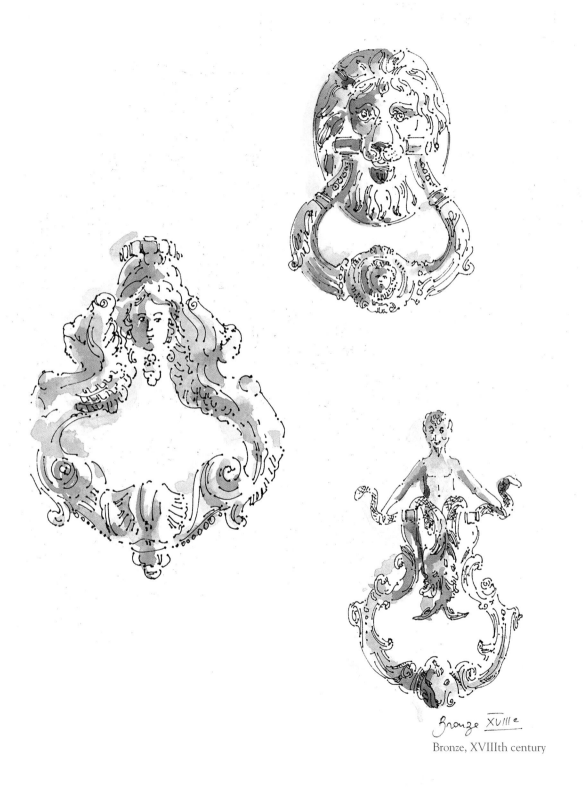

Bronze, XVIIIth century

Door-knockers

DOMINIQUE FERNANDEZ
MÈRE MÉDITERRANÉE

LE VOYAGE
D'ITALIE

Flammarion

Grand Tour

VENISE
Aquarelles de Turner

L'italien
en
10 leçons

à presto !

With all thanks to Patrick Perrin and Véronique Prat, who initiated the project. Also to Alain Flammarion and François-Jean Daehn.

A big Thank you to:

Roger Avque, Estelle Bouchet, Alain Bouldouyre, Francis Blaise, Henri Bouet, Manuel Burrus, Michel Cavendish, Dominique Fernandez, Astrid Kohl, Catherine Laulhère, Sandrine Balihaut-Martin, Olivia Meslay, Alexandra Scarpa, Véronique Lopez, not forgetting Windsor & Newton...

Grazie, finally, to all the friends who opened Italy's doors for me!

Originally published as *Mes Carnets d'Italie*
© Flammarion 2000

English-language edition
© Flammarion 2002

All drawings © FLORINE ASCH

Page 38: quote from Marcel Proust, *The Fugitive*. From *In Search of Lost Time: Swann's Way*. Edited by D.J.Enright, translated by Scott Moncrieff and Kilmartin. Vintage Books, 1996.

Pages 7, 43, and 46: quotes from Paul Morand, *Venices*. Translated by Euan Cameron. London: Pushkin Press, 2002.

Page 54: quote from Valery Larbaud, *Ode*. From "Poems of A.O. Barnabooth: A Selection from Borborgyms." Translated by Alan Jenkins. In *A.O.Barnabooth, His Diary*. Translated by Gilbert Cannan. London: Quartet Books, 1991.

Page 110: Dominique Fernandez, *The Mother Sea*. Translated by Michael Calm. London: Secure & Warburg, 1967.

ISBN: 2-0801-1147-X
FA 1147-02-XII
Dépôt légal: 03/2003

All rights reserved. No part of this publication may be reproduced in any form or by any means, electronic, photocopy, information retrieval system, or otherwise, without written permission from Flammarion.

Printed in Spain by JCG